milk of the tide
poems | leeza jayde

Milk of the Tide

Copyright © 2025 Leeza Jayde

All rights reserved. No part of this publication may be reproduced, distributed, or transmitted in any form or by any means, including photocopying, recording, or other electronic or mechanical methods, without the prior written permission of the author, except in the case of brief quotations embodied in critical reviews and certain other non-commercial uses permitted by copyright law.

Paperback ISBN: 978-0-6451334-5-5
E-book ISBN: 978-0-6451334-4-8

Front cover image by Courtney Errey
Illustrations by Courtney Errey
Cover design by Rachel Kelli
Interior design and typography by Euan Monaghan

First printing edition 2025

for c.w.
the boy who never wore his shoes

the undersea

handheld garden

have you ever smelled rotting flowers?
how they reek of regret and decayed hope.
you can change the water all you want.
still, they wilt. heads bowed under a crown of flies.
weeping petals. staling the air between us.
you might move its corpse to another vase
    but dead is dead.

and that was us, desperately sprinkling sugar
into our glass coffin
while turning our backs to the fact
that we could not revive it.
this handheld garden we had grown together
and eventually left to wither.

leeza jayde

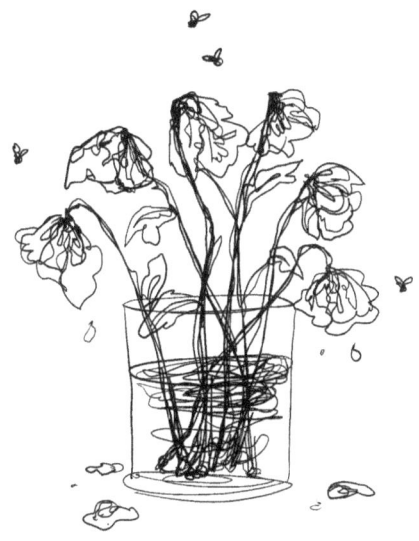

the lake

the ice sings and cracks
beneath my feet.

i cannot help but think if perhaps
this is how it was always supposed to be.

   me
in the middle of the lake.

   you
never able to fully reach me in time.

i grind the memory of us
between my teeth
until all i can taste is ash
whenever i try to say that *i'm over you.*

milk of the tide

birth of a flood

rain droplets lining the bottom layer of a pail.
it feels like nothing at first, but with every *drip*
it becomes something one might drown in.

if i were to lay face down in it,
i could sink.

we do not recognise
the birth of a flood
until it's up to our nose.

until we're inhaling the rain
and it has already found a home
in our lungs.

churches

won't you please tell me if it's all in my mind.
that our interlaced fingers don't feel hollow now?

i cut my hair to my ears and you didn't notice it.
i forget to ask you about your day
and you forget to invite me anywhere.

a door closing. no windows opening.
bulbs flickering.

but if it's all in my head, won't you tell me?
that i'm wrong.
that we're still each other's churches.

that what we have
is just asleep.

false idols

we make gods of people,
stooping down to gently wash their soles.
forgetting that the more power you give someone
the harder your knees bruise when you fall to them.

we do it regardless.
madly. happily. wholeheartedly.

we do it too hastily,
and confuse the worship
for love.

ouroboros

when it's late and i cannot sleep, i pull at threads
that i don't know if i really want the answers to
in the unspooling mess that is my mind.
a line of string being sawed between scissor blades.
i do it anyway.

what if i deserve this?
to hold something shakily and open my palms
just to watch as it slips away without looking back.

i made wounded things of people
because people made a wounded thing of me.
the snake eating its tail. ouroboros.

so maybe i do deserve this.
for hands to unclasp mine and not forgive.
for people to leave
and for nothing like courage or love
or faith to ever fill the cavity
that stays behind.

milk of the tide

when you think of me
do you remember the life
that i brought

or just the falling of leaves
at the end of all things?

everyone else made me feel heavy.
but to you i was something
more than bearable.

i was silk and saffron
and polished abalone shells.

a rare glint.
gold buried beneath topsoil.
worth getting grit under your nails for.

   — wanted

when?

when does a shooting star
become a falling rock?

when does a sparked match
become a wildfire?

when did we
become oil and water
and the holding of breath
until lips turned purple?

the truth tastes like salt snaking down my face.
soft *plinks* against the floorboards at my feet.

holy water coating my lips.
they part and try to speak.
to release me. say it aloud.

but the honesty clots in the column of my throat.
a bullet lodged in the shotgun's barrel-neck.

i cannot answer the question.
it will undo me.

   — do you still love me?

a tapestry of time

i couldn't look the mirror-girl in the eyes
because she was always looking away. refusing
to glance at the way her legs dimpled
with the rolling waves of time.

but i've begun to think it's pretty.
like streams of rainwater
when it runs through riverbeds.

i wish now, as a woman,
that i could hold her in my arms
and trace circles on her palms
the way my mother always did when i was sad.
tell her how beautiful every piece of her is.
a tapestry of time. star dust turned flesh.
the love of two people incarnate.

i wish she could see what i see with older eyes.

when my collar bones are shallow enough
to sip water from like tapered cups,
then will you stay?

if i grind down these thorns
and prune my tongue back
behind my bared teeth,

if i shrink and pluck and dye myself,
when my t-shirts become togas,
and my thighs no longer kiss,

when i file away who i am and
clip these outstretched wings
to fit the narrow mould of self-erasure
society prescribes me,

perhaps then you'll stay.

— an (unhealthy) ode to happiness

kindling

there's a little voice in my head
and i can never seem to silence her whispers.

whenever i accomplish something
she's there, ready, to tear it down.
question it. break it into kindling
and feed it to the flames
of frustration and resentment.

she holds my nose
and makes me swallow sour lies
that i don't believe
until i do.

leeza jayde

the moth and her moon

believing you could change
was a moth thinking
she could reach the moon,
drawn to the glow of silvery light
that could never be touched.

i carried you on my back,
praying the weight
would turn into wings.

but healing is not a gift
you can give to someone
who doesn't want to hold it.

so i flew into the open flame—
because even the pain
felt warmer
than being alone.

excuses

my concept of healthy love
is an orphan.

and it's nobody else's job
to parent it.

i must remind myself
that it's okay that i feel hurt. that i flinch.
but i cannot keep making excuses for myself.
for hiding away when i want more.

i have to want the healing enough
to chase it.

making room

i have this irrational thought
that doesn't feel so irrational.

that if i feel happy and it ends, it'll hurt worse
than if i had just stayed somewhere
between sad and smiling.
and maybe i'm right.

perhaps happiness will not *always* stay,
but i can make better room for it.
i can give it my blessing to bloom.

a spring tree doesn't break under the weight
of all the flowers it births anew;
there is no such thing as too happy.

MY JOY IS NOT
a mayfly.

IT WILL LIVE FOR AS LONG
as i let it.

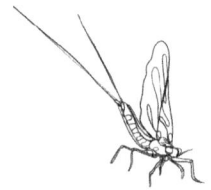

morse code

i'm too young to have lost this much time.
i lose hours to overthinking.
present years to my past.
it's why i can never sit still.

why my leg is always hammering its heel
into the floorboards. a creaking symphony.
bone against skin and skin against wood.
repeat and repeat and repeat and

my fingers are always drumming a solo
on the countertop, on my desk, on my knee.

it's all really just morse code
for my existential anxiety.

pulse

love is no longer enough
when you cut yourself on each other's words
and apologies are just husks.
love is not enough when trust is broken
and it cannot be remade. when the rust settles in.

when the nights are sleepless and the job is thankless
and your needs are not also equally met.
when your sorrow does not move them
the way it once did. when appreciation dies.

when you give more than you get.
when you grow apart.

love is just not enough when you cannot find
the pulse of it in the one you care for anymore.

afraid

i have given my time to people
who tucked my dreams into their back pockets.
who penciled their support into calendars
and never got around to it.
who my sadness was an inconvenience for.
and, despite that i deserved better, i stayed.

sometimes we're afraid of better.
of what love that listens—truly listens—feels like.

milk of the tide

i watch our love story through my fingers now,
and i can barely stand to look,
knowing what was yet to come.

shipwreck

i was the nearest life raft in a roaring tempest
and you clung on for dear life.

it felt dizzying, to be wanted.
you poured saltwater and i drank.

so it was an axe to the boat's hull
when you said you didn't need me anymore.

this is how he leaves

he sits across the table from me.
down he reaches, sliding out a prepared list
from his breast pocket.
it dangles just short of his lap.
he is nothing if not organised.

he recites carefully crafted dot points
of everything that i failed to be.
each line slices, flays back the skin
of all of my old insecurities.
he lays them bare. but i am too in love
to call it cruelty.

i do not cry, and for this i'm proud.
when i ask if we can still be friends,
he pats my arm. tells me i couldn't handle that.

in his eyes, i am a sparrow's egg,
already half-cracked and leaking yolk,
and i am too lost now
to call it condescension.

leeza jayde

YOU WERE AN OPEN CUT
for so long.

EVERY *SORRY* SPOKEN
was shaped like shame.

all teeth

you did not name her
amongst the reasons why you left
but i would learn about it later.

i begged the silence
when you drove away that day
for a softer knife, and a smaller scar.

you were not as kind
as you thought you were.

i saw your smile in the side mirror
as the car door slammed closed.
all teeth and honeyed relief.

and the summer didn't hold its breath
for my pain or all the days
that i couldn't stomach food thereafter.
it carried on, as you did.

you are not even in the room

my heart still stutters when it hears your name.
these legs liquefy and my breath
becomes a baby's rattle.

it's been months.
you should not still have this hold over me
when you are not even in the room.

the afternoon

it's like when my cat chases the sun
from room to room
to lounge in its shifting light.

i fell for an hour of you
that only shows its face
when the clouds disperse.
warm and bright—and temporary.

i fell in love with the afternoon.

slow work

what we had wasn't healthy
and it's left creases in my life.

i look for the door now when people are kind
because my mind cannot help
but wonder what they want from me.

when a favour is done for me,
i pay it back tenfold
so i don't owe anybody *anything*.

this is not living. it's surviving.
and you did that to me.

now i am unlearning too much too quickly.
tripping over my feet in impatience to heal.

such slow work—not pulling out stitches
before the wound is sealed.

milk of the tide

you have a switchblade-sharp tongue
behind that cloying smile
and every word tears.

we are an open gash
puckering white at the edges,
and your empty promises
are salt peppered in it.

milk of the tide

obsidian, steel pillars,
the ice-crust of a winter forest lake
and seeing you with her.

you both rehearsing stoic indifference
to my existence
like it's a role you were born to play
when we pass each other in the public spaces
you and i once haunted.

— things that are hard

leeza jayde

HOW EFFORTLESS
it is for you now
TO ERASE ME
from your memory.

IT'S AS IF I WERE
sidewalk chalk
AND YOUR GOODBYE
became the rain.

milk of the tide

i had no say in my funeral

your lips are too easily forgetting the taste of my name
but it doesn't bother you like it bothers me.

i don't want cobwebs to settle over who we were.
can't stand the thought of layers of dust caking
the memory of the way you always moved
into the groove of my neck.
i was once your hiding place.

now you're already filling in my grave.
already whispering a rehearsed eulogy
to every friend asking *why*.

they echo it to me and each lied syllable
is a quiet thunderclap between the ribs.

star hopping

tell me again about how you loved it when
i showed you how to work a telescope. how to
map and trace the stars across the night's navy sea.

suns fell for us that evening. do you remember?
i counted six shooting stars
before you walked me home and finally
after three years of never quite
getting the timing right,
you kissed me
and i felt like i'd never die.
like existing had no great weight to it.

we were like those shooting stars, you and i.
burning bright and loudly
before winking out to black.

i know it's selfish but

i don't know whether to stay—or go.
those eyes are caverns i'd like to shine a torch to.

you're a lot gentler up close. i never knew.
and sometimes, when your eyes are closed,
while i'm in the halfway house between your arms,
i like to pretend you're mine.

this won't last. we're just sugar in hot water.
newspaper left outside in a storm.
i should leave, really. really, i should.

let this poem be a sarcophagus
for everything we never had.

almost-nearly

i've scoured the dictionary
and i can't find a name for what we were.
we were *almost*, but not quite.
nearly, but not enough.

how can i let go of something
i never really had?

the reality is absinthe.
a bitter swallow and intoxicating.
i'd rather have had you and lost you
than drift lost in this fog of what-ifs.

a broken bone is a named pain,
but what were we?

now i'm mourning a future i never had by candlelight.
a vigil in tepid bathwater as i scrub the memory of you
from my skin. as i numbly exfoliate this *almost-nearly*
we never had a name for from every pore.

the girl

egg-shell thin willpower.
you pressed a love bomb between my teeth
and i chewed. a pill i'd hoped would heal me.

i have always been a walking love letter
and you were a promise made in the dark
with crossed fingers.

it was kissing a sunset and pulling teeth.
equal measure of pain and pleasure.
leaving was a lightning strike before the rain.

i hope you said sorry
to the girl you didn't tell me about.

belladonna

how i feel for you
tugs at the concealed seams of me.
i come undone.

a quiet push-pull of something
that i cannot name anymore.
this toxic cocktail of loving and loathing.

my want for you
is belladonna in full bloom.

every memory is a poisoned sip
that sirens me into the velvet drag
of days spent sleeping.

hopscotch

i skip from square to square,
chalk dust powdering my shoes.
my loneliness is a wolf snapping at my ankles.

i have nothing kind to gift myself
so i seek morsels of validation in others.
mistake their arms for anchors. again and again.

a well of love within me but i keep pouring
into empty cisterns.
it leaves me aching and thirsty every time.

i keep seeing edens
in gethsemenes.

instinct

sparrows know to fly south for the winter.
spiderlings know to spin silk patterns,
salmon know to swim upstream,
and this knot in my throat knows
that you will be the death of me.

still, i leave the door unlocked.

i cannot take it with me

the corridors of my skull are choked
with conversations i can't unsay
and return to ad nauseam.

i lie awake at night sleeplessly tracing
the formless bruise of all my regrets.

but what good is this ceaseless gnawing?

all this anxiety
just to not take it with me when i go.

all this living on the periphery
only to leave it behind one day.

the many silhouettes of pain

i wished that the sting of love's end
was the sharpest knife-point i would ever feel.
but as the sun climbs,
it casts long shadows.
pain comes in many silhouettes.
to live is to learn them all.

milk of the tide

i don't know when it began—
jiggling the door handle one too many times
triple checking the lock.
reaching the driveway only to sprint back
to see if the stove is still alight or not.

it started without ceremony or fanfare.
the quiet hums with this cruel ringing
of imagined disaster and
i cannot turn it off.

ocd

when i was twenty, i nearly crashed my car.
it had flaking paint and a finicky volume dial.
i couldn't get it to stay at exactly 22,
and it had to, or i couldn't focus.

odd numbers are evil,
but i couldn't tell you why.
hours sacrificed to unfolding
and re-folding laundry.
placing colour-coded socks into perfect pairs.
hands scrubbed raw, cracked open
like fissuring fault lines
until not a speck remains on my skin.

i don't want these thoughts. they arrive uninvited
and stick like cobwebs in corners i can't reach.
circling, spinning, tightening. never loosening.
to be awake now is to be acutely aware
of every breath, blink and swallow.

i am exhausted daily by noon.

milk of the tide

it's sisyphus rolling his stone.
overthink overthink *overthink*.

you don't understand, i tell my friend
who laughs dismissively at the way
my skin crawls when she scatters
the neat phalanx of pencils on my desk.
whose eyes narrow when my fingers
twitch to move them back into formation.

— *i'm just trying to survive*

veneer

this attention to detail is a disease.
i line up pens, plates, shoes
until the rows are perfect.

order is momentary chamomile
for what others stole from me:
stability and predictability i was denied.
this veneer of control is my cane.

i am not ignorant to this excess,
but if the dishes stay dirty,
if the smudge is not wiped,
my brain screams an air-raid siren
nobody else can hear.

loop

sometimes i'll get a thought and it sticks.
a carousel that never slows to let me off.
the loop is both the cage and the lock.

      spinning
    spinning   spinning
   spinning   spinning
spinning   spinning
  spinning   spinning
   spinning spinning
     spinning

it never stops.

homesick – part i

i'm homesick for a memory
i wish i'd lived longer in.

gardening in the spring with nanna.
after hours of tending to the roses so gently
you'd think them hospital patients,
we'd slouch into our armchairs and sigh.

my grandfather would wander on in from his shed,
hands cracked from hard work,
and ruffle my hair.

nanna would set jellies in the shape of a cottontail.
i always felt guilty when i scooped a spoonful
of its wobbly ears, and my grandparents
would both laugh at my childishness.
and i'd smile because i simply liked
the sound of their happiness in the air.

homesick – part ii

we'd watch wayne sling guns and jones find the
treasure and my grandfather would
mouth along to the words,
perched on the edge of his seat even though he'd
seen these films a hundred times before.

he could find wonder in something
that he knew every line to.

i still sit in his chair sometimes
and close my eyes.
pretend he's still tousling my hair.

leeza jayde

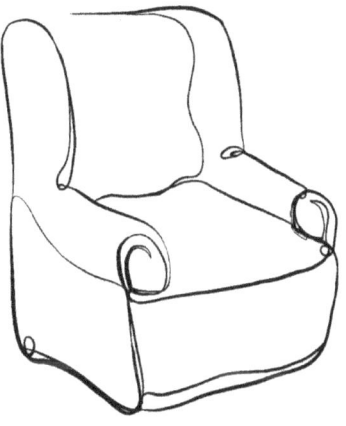

alzheimer's

to make dust of dreams.
fumble for memories that have dissolved away.
to forget your friends, your children's names.
what happened only yesterday.
how to eat, swallow. breathe.
a maddening, unwilling slipping into sleep.
to go before you should.

to go before you should.

the magic of salt

i thought it strange.
how healing often stings
right before the growth happens,
and often involves salt.

the ocean air burns my lungs
when every breath is already an ache
but fire-glow sunsets over sea waves
temporarily lulls my sorrow.

and the brininess of the names
that i grieve and release in these tears
renews me.

WHAT HURTS
is what cleanses us.

WHAT LEAVES
can make room.

the undersea

light dissolves down here.
and it is so quiet that i can finally
hear myself think.

in the weightlessness of numbed floating,
i learn the new shape of myself.

my sadness becomes a space
where i can grow through the pulsing
of all this pain. i am becoming.

i think nothing is ever wasted unless we let it be.
and i will let all this aching teach me something.

*to rise
after sinking*

hindsight

we existed in pockets of sun together.
campfires, croaked laughter from overuse,
ride-on mowers careening in the paddock.

finding field dirt in our socks for days afterwards.
hollering under the fingernail moon as a pack.
life was slow and warm and whole.

we had no idea that we would lose you.

for some, it numbs.
antarctica in the bloodstream.
snow not even the sun can soften.
it lives within.

for others, it twists them up.
a seed flowering weeds.

it takes every good thing
and turns it to firewood.

— grief

milk of the tide

closure is nervous sparrow
constantly taking flight
before i can catch it.

i beg it to stay
but on my terms and timing.

i claw at it, trying too hard
to hold its little heartbeat in my hands
but i am impatient with it,
angry with it,
and it will not stay.

these palms are not open perches.
they closed, clenched fists.

there is nowhere safe
for it to nest.

you do not go, we do not miss you

in the hush-theatre of my mind,
we still speak.
you feign interest in brontë novels for my sake;
in return, i nod about the engines you pry apart,
oily and gleaming like opened fruit.

in the sanctuary of my mind,
the last time we speak isn't in my hallway,
and i am not complaining about overdue essays
i have yet scrawl a grade on.

in this re-cut reel, when you hug me too tightly,
it feels strange and i pay attention.
when you say goodbye,
i notice the hitch in your voice.
i call you afterwards and you answer.

you never get in the car.
there is no shattering of glass.
no silence thereafter.

milk of the tide

you do not go, we do not miss you.
here, in my mind, you are kept safe
from the night that took you from us.

my fingertips will never forget the memory
of unpinching a flower sprig
and letting it fall down onto your coffin.
a wilted poppy landing on the closed lid.

it didn't even make a sound.

you won't know

october 7th is the longest day
in our calendar year.

you didn't understand
how deeply loved you were.
are still.

if only you knew
how we still see you
on the couch, in the shed,
in our hallways, rooms and
in the passenger seat.
how we quote the comical things
you'd say on the daily.

there are footprints
of you everywhere
that not even the waves
can wash away.

milk of the tide

leeza jayde

i remember so much about you.
you never wore shoes or took off your cap.
when you smiled, you were kind and creased eyes
and your laugh broke the sound barrier.

you had a heart like duck down.
like dandelion kisses,
with arms that were just as soft and gentle
and quiet to land in.

— *c.w.*

milk of the tide

I CAN'T TURN
water into wine.

I CAN'T MOVE
the mountain stone.

I CAN'T PART
the red sea.

I CAN'T BRING
you back home.

leeza jayde

unravelling

mourning is a journey with no map or compass
or road signs. clocks are irrelevant.

the unbraiding of a tangled thread. unravelling
a frayed knot just to find another. and another.
and more still—and a mountain of rope yet to go.

it's about them and the space they left,
but it's also learning who you are without them.
everything left unspoken.

ripples

unclasp your watch and let yourself feel, remember.
hold a watering can to your heart and sprinkle seeds.
keep at it until the flowers one day wake up again.

i don't think the ache ever fully fades.
they will always be a part of you
as long as you carry their love.

it takes someone very special
to leave ripples behind.

milk of the tide

when you found me, i was a closed off room
but you took a hairpin to my locks.

you handed me a pair of scissors
in the grocery carpark and told me
to cut your hair. so i did.
in front of all that traffic, i cut a girl's hair
who trusted me completely.
strands sailed away in the wind
and i felt myself grow lighter.

being friends with you
is laying in a field of lavender
when the world is too loud.
it's everyone thinking we're sisters
and you remembering my favourite things.
it's unspoken love in every
text me when you get home
and *come here* before you
pull me into a long hug.

— how she helped save me

leeza jayde

why i thank god for her

— she sucks back coffee like it's medicine
— when she smiles, she shows all her teeth
— she brought me 1am flowers when my friend died
  and i slept that night feeling broken, but loved
— her compliments are never laced with envy
— life has split and re-split her knuckles yet
  she has used every lesson to help others
— she is fluent in forgiveness
— secrets glide through her ears but never out her lips
— she is the kind of friend i never knew i needed

she, a pillar of strength

once, my friend worked for over a month
without realising she had a broken rib,
her silent strength always moving.

she is the steel skeleton of the house
that her siblings live so safely inside of,
and even when her bad ankles buckle,
she threads her fingers through others'
and helps them to stand—and rise.

to know her is to be a witness to quiet strength
that doesn't ask for attention,
yet shifts the weight of the lives around her.

a plea to my sisterhood friends

please prune my thorns
and slip me back in water.
kick sand over the flames when they
skirt too close to the woods.
throw a knee-rug over the glass
that encircles me so i might tentatively tread
over to your open arms.

i know i am not always gentle.
life has not always been gentle with me,
so i'm clumsy with it sometimes.
a newborn to vulnerability and trust.

all this to say, please, won't you stay
while i'm learning gentle?

while i'm unlearning all this hurt.

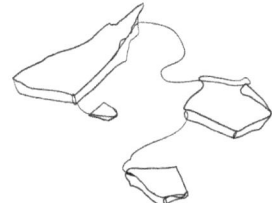

this made me think of you

such a warm string of syllables to receive.
to think that you find me in things
that make you pause. make you stop and notice.
that i also fall into that category. noticed. *seen*.
to flit into your head the way one might
come and go into a house as they please.
you gave me the spare key.

this is the closest thing i've come to poetry
in someone else's mouth.

leeza jayde

what a
MEDICINE
it is

to call you
MY FRIEND.

the midas touch

you've got the midas touch, they tell me.

turning all this pain to gold.

but they do not see the way
my pen shakes when i write.

to scribe it all down is not always to build
a monument of the aching.

i do not always feel so sage.

to hurt is to learn to live with it. hear it out.

to release it.

knocking

what a slippery thing this healing is.
like mist. fog. northern lights.
i stretch for it and it dances out of reach.
a flirt, a sneak. it evades me.
and besides,
i'm a coward.
because i'm scared of what will happen
when i heal.

when anger isn't my sword
and my ribs are not a wall.
when i let the light in.
feel what warmth is again.
when i am vulnerable.

when i open the door and let hope greet me.

i can feel it knocking.

sabotage

to rob someone of their healing
is to cradle them past the point of growth.

do not coddle your partner.
you are not their parent.

to walk beside
is tenderness,
but to carry
is disservice.

you can call it love all you like.
it will still be unwitting sabotage.

the quiet you inherited

you wear your hurt like chains.
i cannot hear your thoughts,
and it makes you frustrated.
an inner child reaching for a language
they were never taught.

you slam doors like punctuation,
leave bite-marks in the air because
no one showed you
how to build a sentence
that holds its weight without breaking.
your parents spoke in hurricanes
or not at all.

and i—
i am so tired of translating.
it is exhausting, deciphering
your intentions.

our love is choking,
not for lack of heat,
but for want of words.

how one becomes a black hole

fold into yourself. burn bright and hot
and then, just when things couldn't get any worse—
and they do (of course they do)—
collapse in on yourself. become star debris.
drift in the dust belt of your misery.

where light used to live, eat everything
that comes within your pull. drain it. consume.
die a little inside and don't work to heal.
don't help yourself.
do *nothing*.

do nothing at all.

the goldilocks zone

it's safer for me here,
living in a stretch of space where
you don't see me often enough to notice my flaws,
and not too little enough to lose interest entirely.

you think i'm playing hard to get,
but it's not that at all.

i don't know if i'm anything less than too much
or anything more than not enough.
it's all i was ever told.

i've never known who i am
except through someone else's eyes.

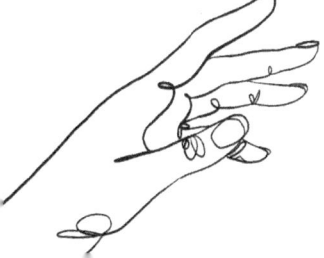

galatea and pygmalion

i keep having the dream where i'm made of clay.
soft and passive enough to shape.

every night, hands find me,
sculpting, chiselling, choosing.
they tell me who to be and
i let them.

but i never quite look like the way i feel.

that's the part that always makes me wake
and lie still until the sun spills
over the lip of my windowsill,
wondering if there's anything left of me
that is still mine.

breaking rituals

they say to start small.
my finger spasms to lift the tea towel.
to fold it into a perfect rectangle.
leaving it scrunched is alarm bells
and clammy palms.

to name the pain is to dull its teeth
through understanding that its bite serves a purpose.
so i keep trying little things.
touching a doorknob only once and walking away.

it is agony.
yet each refusal plants
roots of courage that twist
in the dark, hungry for the sun.

these rituals. my body's frantic inventions
to keep me safe.
they will not vanish overnight.
but healing, even slow,
is still healing.

i never told my friends, but they knew

they only ever saw me tap my knees
an even amount of times
(except in multiples of five).

when they reached to hold my hand
it was always a struggle to let someone
touch my skin without seeking out soap.

i never told my friends
because i didn't have to.

they welcomed me as i am
and let me work on myself
at my own pace
with grace
and without shame.

your past makes you
RELATABLE.

every mistake makes you
HUMAN.

how we stopped my watch

do you ever think about me anymore?
you used to be here all the time.
love has a lifespan. i know that.
and, yet, i can't help myself.
it kills me never knowing
all your secrets now.

my mirror's clothed in faded polaroids.
i peel them off,
but can't throw them away.
shoulders pressed together.
cheek to cheek.
so much laughter
frozen in a flash.

leeza jayde

i want to hate you, but i don't think that's fair

because everything ends. i prayed until my knees
unbearably chafed that we would make it.
desperately, i needed us to.
dying embers died early, and i held onto a
yearning ghost of what we once were.

i wanted to loathe you for leaving, but
more so for leaving me to drown alone.

seeing you with her is greek fire to a home we built.
of course you deserved happiness, but the body wasn't yet
rigid. it was still warm—and starving. but the cold
reality is that we didn't know what we were doing.

you and i both look happier now, i think.

isn't it funny? how friends become

loves and loves become strangers.
on and on the world goes but we
venture, strive, *pray* to forget. yet
every now and then, i remember us.
do you? would you if you let yourself?

years blur by. the memories
only fray at the edges a little.
under different circumstances, maybe.

   — maybe we'd still be friends

bird-egg love

they do not deserve you. so let them go.
you are not a late night bar brag.
not another notch in their bedpost.

you are a universe of emotion.
of hopes, wants, dreams, stories.
you deserve more than what they can give you.
so offer them nothing more.

i know it's painful. the fact that you even care at all
after everything is a testament to the bird-egg love
you hold in your palms, that you offer up so willingly.

so, yes, it will hurt. it will continue to. for a while.
but it will be worth it when you can look back
and they are a speck in the distance.
an atom in your solar system.

let them go so you can hold onto something better.
they couldn't gift it to you, so gift it to yourself.

let them go. let them go.

eyes closed

coastal erosion.
the slow crumbling of cliffside bone,
each piece yielding to the sea.

i'm not the coast in this analogy,
or the storm, or the cliff-edge house
clinging to its last breath.

i am the tenant who won't abandon her home.
who hears the groaning shift of soil,
and stays anyway. loyal to the end.
eyes closed, waiting for the sea to take me
and whatever remains of us.

you'll move on

what if i don't want to forget?
if the mountain between me and growth
is being neck-deep in memories
that only one of us will keep alive,
then let me just resuscitate it a little longer.
let me miss you a little harder
before i let you go.

leeza jayde

the strength others now witness
VEILS THE QUIET WARS
that it took
TO BECOME YOU.

milk of the tide

leeza jayde

somewhere to stay

the house i was raised in backed onto a meadow,
a field that yellowed in the cold season.
when the rains came, so did the mice.

i could never bring myself to kill them.
not them, with their little whiskers and big eyes,
nor the slow hobbling beetle,
nor the skinny spider weaving out of hunger
in the corners of our hallway
for flies that would not come.

i cupped them in bowls like held breath,
and patiently returned them to the outside,
hiding them under leaves and sticks
or in the abandoned backyard shed.

i have never harboured qualms with creatures,
simply begging for warmth—or shelter.

their desperation is a kind of innocence
that i cannot turn away from.

firefly

i can feel hope's breath on my neck.
it murmurs promises of more than this
into the shell of my ear.

but to move on is to free
the flickering firefly
caged in my cupped palms.

i don't know if i can do that,
when all the memories i have
are the only evidence we ever existed.
but i know i must.

leeza jayde

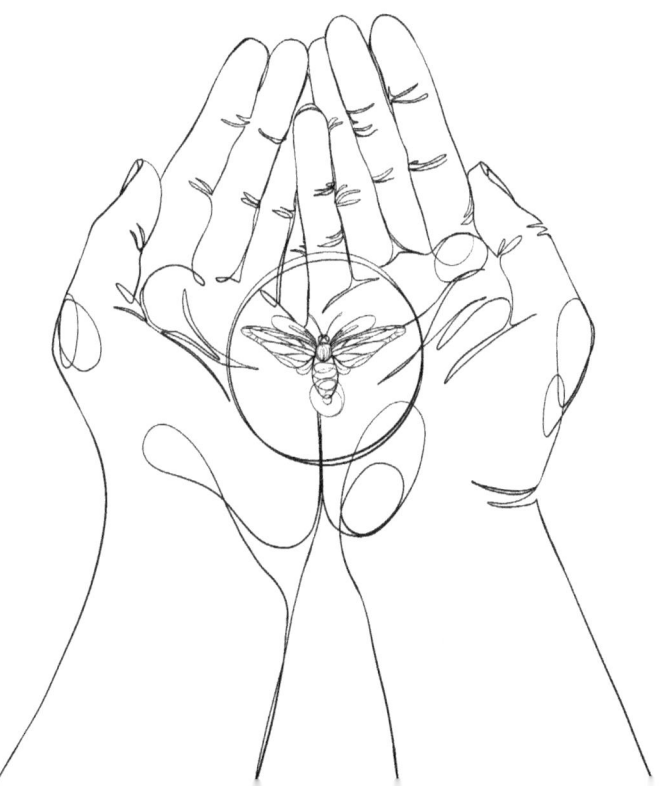

rabbit's ears

boys have only ever held me like they were hungry,
but your hands were clouds. cotton. rabbit's ears.
a child's breath when they whisper and sunlight
when it falls on flowers.

you were gentle in a barbed-wire world.
and even though we didn't last,
i will always thank you for that.

leeza jayde

handprints

you were a pause. a beat.
a blissful breath between surviving
and learning how to heal and move on.
for a time, you were my shelter.

the truth is not everyone we have feelings for
is who we are meant to be with,
but they leave handprints in the wet cement
of who we grow into.
they do not pass through our lives
without echo, and they do not leave us
empty-handed.

you deserve nothing less

you chased a girl opposite to me in every way,
in the sense that she wouldn't break your heart.

you were snow that melted in my hands.
and she is winter draped in white.

it brings me great comfort knowing
that she loves you in all the ways
i didn't know how.

milk of the tide

you are never coming back.

our hourglass ran out.
short but sweet.

but underneath all this sadness,
i smile.

i cannot help but feel glad you were here
even if it was just for
a little while.

leeza jayde

i am too young for this

adrenaline rushes daily through these tired veins.
my heart runs marathons over the years.
hardly resting. racing.
fight or flight becomes my normalcy.
i am almost never still.

by the time i am twenty,
it needs to nap—
pauses for a few seconds,
then stutters back to life.

i close my eyes as my skull
meets a cold *crack* against the table.

milk of the tide

the hospital is thick with sterile white
and blindingly clinical.
i am kept for hours.
scans. clipboards. a wrap-around monitor
is a parting present i must return tomorrow.

if i am fortunate, they say that i will not
need a pacemaker for a while.
they are hopeful.

the treatment is simple now;
i must take better care of myself.
not just the version of me others see,
but the me who i live with privately.

you don't look sick

i cancel plans again
and pray my friends don't find me fickle.

tomorrow, i will go to work anyway.
rent doesn't grieve for swollen organs.

in meetings, i nod, smile. all the while
the pain lights matchsticks
beneath my skin, and the room
blurs at the edges like a dream and spins.

i still laugh, still pin my hair back,
and sweep on mascara
to paint pretty over the strain.

you don't look sick, they say,
as if i have not had to learn
to fight through it
and just go about my every day.

milk of the tide

just because
IT ISN'T SEEN

doesn't mean it doesn't
BLISTER, BRUISE OR BLEED.

pain is pain is pain.

my body is a battleground
where illness both gnaws away at me
and swells all the same.

the world's gaze
is not kind to women
who dress for comfort.

service comes with bigger smiles
when our stomachs aren't bloated.

i wonder if they ever
see me for me
or just the shape
i shift between.

this body

she is a sanctuary.
a place of soft strength.

i am not dressed for your eyes
or anyone's but mine.

this body is my home
and you must knock and be invited
before you are welcomed
to look in through the windows.

leeza jayde

to be a woman in a world of wolves

weld your lips together and smile
when a fire is burning your throat.
eat the smoke. chew. swallow.
let him speak. good girl.
soften your spine. be silent
when you want to scream.

don't go jogging with a ponytail.
it's too easy to grab.
shrink yourself. smile more. eat less.
don't interrupt him, sweetheart.

clutch your keys like weapons
on the way to your parked car after night shifts.
text *are you home safely?* like a prayer.
fake being on the phone
so they'll leave us alone.

that is part of being a woman
in a world of wolves.

breadcrumbs

i spent too much time listening to my anxiety
instead of understanding her.

i tried to follow her turtles all the way down
when i could have questioned why she does
the things that she does.

but i never bothered following the breadcrumbs
she left me, trying to lead me home to myself.
and i could have.

i could have been kinder.

leeza jayde

to rise after sinking

it all weighs me down.
tethers me to the ocean floor.

i have carried them for so long—
all of these stones in my shoe.
each one a name, a mistake, a grief.
ghosts of things unsaid. and pain
swallowed instead of spoken.

i have walked with it all for so long.
limping became familiar.
the sinking, a surrender.
the weight, second nature.

now i pry them out.
i press each one to my lips.
release them, and
stone by stone,
i begin to rise.

milk of the tide

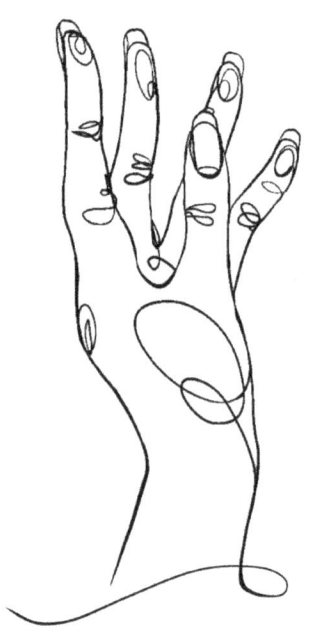

*milk of
the tide*

the lighthouse

the lighthouse—that's what they call you.
you feel as though you can never
dim the bulb. rest. people need you
to guide them to shore. it is a privilege
to be the anchor for the ones you love. it is.
but the carer needs to be cared for.
the arms that hold need to be held too.

you must be your own lighthouse
before anybody else's, or the glow
will burn out altogether.

leeza jayde

rebuilding from ruins

what if i tore down this house?
what if i rebuilt from the wreckage
and put up walls with windows
that face the sun? formed doors that
did more than lock me in
when i closed them and rooms
that weren't quite so cluttered?

what if i took all this pain and used it
to help others grow through
what they're going through?

and what if i sat down and decided
i wanted more than this?

the hideaway

your sigh against my neck.
the safe place you'd hide after a long day.
that's what i miss the most.
being the hideaway for someone else.
trusted and special. a home.

but i will become this again.
if not for someone else, then for myself.
and this will need to be enough.

forward

i type the texts just to never send them.
but not everything i hide can be hidden.
my body still sighs,
and my smiles don't reach my eyes.

i can never go back to who i was before we met.
so know that i will not look back for you.

my feet only know forward now.

coupe de grâce

this strawberry-red lipstick.
the coup de grâce to your last hope
that i am somehow sadder without you here.

i'm not.

you left to break me, a punishment,
but i have never felt more like myself.

when the last dregs of lonely left me,
i felt alive again. unshaken
and with room to grow.

oxytocin

don't text me later than you could have
because your friends told you that
it'll stoke the ember in my chest.
they're wrong.
it flickers out too easily these days.

my trust is sand slipping through fingers,
but we could make castles out of it,
away from the sea and wind,
where they could keep.
we could mould a kingdom.

tell me you're thinking about me
or leave me be entirely.
i have only so much oxytocin
left in my life to feel.
it is not a plaything to spill at your feet.
i have no time for games of give and take.

i will speak

i will speak even if my voice
arrives in splinters behind my teeth.

let it crack with emotion.
porcelain syllables.
the sound means the words
were born of my marrow.

all the things worth saying
often begin as whispers
buried in the throat.

i have spent too long
choking on my silence
thinking it might make me likeable.

no more.
i will fill the air with all
that once kept me small.

leeza jayde

shook the seeds

you left before the first bloom of my spring.
before the petals unfurled and shook off
the snow-kissed dustings of winter.
and so, now you will never know the way
i stretch towards warmth. how i am so
tenderly gentle and bursting with love.

you were the storm that shook
the seeds to the surface. that is to say,
your leaving made space for my becoming.
you helped me find her. this new me.
but i did the growing.

not every weed should be pulled.
you were a part of my journey.

i wish you well.

i long for

someone who will love me
like when my mother would warm my towels
in our old tumble dryer on cold nights,
or how my dad would buckle me in with bedsheets
and leave the citrusy glow of a lamp on
when i was scared.
the way nanna carefully peeled my oranges
to remove every string of pith
so i might enjoy the taste to its fullness.

a love like forehead kisses, extra honey in my tea.
just to be thought of often—and fondly.

a love where ego dies and care is unfiltered.
a love that meets me every day
in small, unspoken ways.

i am finally
SETTLED AT HOME
within the walls of myself.

a love letter to my solitude

i tug the turtleneck over my head
and wrap myself in the snug hush
of my ivory coat before stepping into the rain.

i jump in puddles just to hear the splash
and pluck a solitary flower
from the cracks in the pavement
and tuck it into my hair.

i buy myself that new book i wanted;
watch a movie i've been meaning to see.
alone but not lonely.

home waits for me with the lights on.
just the way i left it. this is safety. comfort.

i unclip my hair, and brush it
because it deserves to be touched
by someone who loves
the way it feels.

a candlelit bath red-flecked
with loose flower petals.
white satin robe. a dance in the kitchen,
barefoot, as pasta boils.
i stopped counting calories.
i'm happy as i am.

the kettle sings along with me.
i make tea just the way i like it.
manuka honey. steeped, strong and minty.

i sprawl across my queen bed,
take up all the space i want now
that i have more room for me.

milk of the tide

i show up for myself every day.
make breakfast, fold fresh laundry, stack dishes,
all so i won't need to do it later.

i sip water and start my day
with quiet little moments
so as not to overwhelm myself.

i smooth cream into my dry hands
and rub my feet when they ache.

i love myself in all the small, tender ways
that i can. this is caring for myself.

it has become as natural as breathing air.
a routine, this self-care.

the romance of routine

the mundane is only mundane
because i do it so often,
and that's how i know that i love me.

i read because it brings me peace,
wrap myself in sweaters when it's cold,
make myself warm meals when i'm hungry.

i am here. i stay. i show up for myself
with all the gentleness that i was denied.

one way window

we make idols of those
who will never know our names.
peering into glass screens.
a one way window.
looking into lives that aren't ours,
hoping it might fill the quiet.

bell jar

you're missing so many noticings.
please, put the screen down.
let silence breathe. your world
was never meant to be loud
all of the time.

plugged in
but so disconnected.
instant sugar
replaced the slow chew.

how can you hear
the real world's magic
when you so willingly coil
yourself inside this bell jar
of ceaseless static?

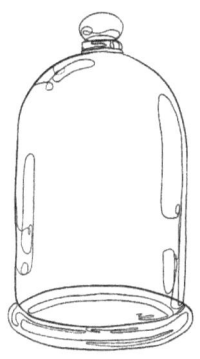

places we forget

nature looks beautiful
when someone you loved
has gone home to it.

laughing children will move you
when you remember
we are not born hating others.

smiling at strangers isn't awkward
when you could be their only proof
that kindness exists today.

light lives quietly
in all of the places
we forget to look.

leeza jayde

please read this at my funeral

i will miss the way sunlight dapples across
my grey reading chair
at five o'clock in the afternoon.
the smell of new books (or old ones).
freshly cut watermelon in summer
and swaying in my egg chair
when the world feels too much.

i will miss my best friends' tight embraces
and fresh sheets on rainy nights.
i will miss the way someone tastes my name
for the very first time.
laughing myself sick with my mother.
sharing stillness with dad when we paint.

the world will keep on spinning
and somewhere, at five o'clock in the afternoon
the sun will find my chair again.

i hope you'll remember me
in small and tender things.

bone china girl

sometimes i forget that i am a sensitive person.
that i am made of soft things.

i am the type who,
when she sees someone cry,
turns to bone china
and reflexively reaches for their hand.

i know no other way to be
besides arms open
and unguarded.

leeza jayde

today, i crushed a small garden snail
underneath my gumboot.
its little curled house cracked like a knuckle.
i went quiet all afternoon.

it was an accident.
i have made many.
and i care, deeply, desperately,
about them all.

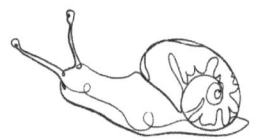

i have bruised others, and these hands
are so lead-heavy with apologies.

leeza jayde

hungry people lick whatever crumbs
they are handed.

fish don't know the bait is hooked.
deer don't see the bullet coming.

it was not your fault.

offer yourself permission
to be human.

now you know better.

so you owe it to yourself
to disappoint the people
who expect to see you
stay down.

it's never too late
to get back up.

healing isn't a
STRAIGHT LINE.

give yourself grace
TO STUMBLE AND SIDESTEP.

being with someone else
after learning your boundaries
is like being reborn.

when you feed yourself
self-love, you don't need
the compliments or
to please others.

you are not responsible
for their happiness.
nor are they
for yours.

leeza jayde

i am terrified of heights

but i board the plane regardless.
my friends and this new country
are a remedy today.

as we soar over rainforests,
i shout to the sky
and it's swallowed by a laugh.

i bathe in warm springs and drink
spring water so crisp that i gasp.
when strangers make conversation
while we wait for drinks, i smile
instead of shrink into myself.
we pedal through the streets of rotorua
until our legs throb and it feels like i'm flying.

franz josef is snow-capped. quiet and peaceful,
and there is a childlike wonder in me
that flickers when we see the blue glow
of the waitomo caves.

i do not recognise this version of myself.
here, i stand in the stillness of her.

healing

there's alchemy in laughing
until your temples throb at 2am
with friends in a foreign town.

in those moments, the pain is uninvited.
it is uncomfortable with your happiness
and leaves the room.
here, there is a blissful pause
in your heartbreak.

the aching is swallowed by the smiling.
whispered secrets make you feel seen
and there is a remedial warmth
in each other's company.

i am more than

my trembling hands
and moments of human weakness.

than when grief curled me fetal.
and people pinched me in soft places.

i am more than a mosaic
of what others have done to me.

milk of the tide

eucalyptus

my fingers drag across the bark.
rough, ruptured and blackened with soot.
the eucalyptus stands, skeletal,
singed by one of the worst fires
we've seen for years here.

my teacher once told me
that they need flames to open.
the ash is the cradle
for new seeds to release.

people aren't so different.
we burn before we bloom.
in the blistering, something is born.

and beneath complete ruin,
a bud, green and stubborn,
wiggles its way
to the topsoil.

goodbye to the girl

gone is the never wading deeper
than where my toes can kiss the sand
beneath the waves.

gone is the girl
who thought feeling too much
made her less loveable,
who bit her tongue all the time.

i am trying new things, bold things,
terrifying things.

staying, or going, or breaking
isn't quite as scary when
it's all happened before.

if i cry, let it be loud.

let it mean something
while i'm still here.

not quite freedom

once, the bed had to be left perfect.
sheets flat, pillows fluffed,
blankets military-tucked.

today, i leave the linen tangled
in a rush to work
and the world doesn't end.

when i lock the door,
one click is enough.

things do not
have to be perfect anymore.

this isn't quite freedom yet,
but it's something like it—
a loosening,
a soft, steady reclaiming.

my mother's skin

my mother takes my hand
and guides it to her stomach.

you lived here once, she says.
every ripple is a reminder
that under her skin was my first home.

her body wove me, sheltered me,
fed me, warmed me.

i owe everything to my mother
and every stippled line in her skin.

i am my cat's whole world

when i come home and she trills,
bounding down the hallway like a song,
when she gazes up at me,
those eyes wide with unblinking trust
and tucks herself into my arms,
i remember she is a brief
yet fulfilling part of my story
but i am her entire life.

how humbling it is to be the
safe place and best friend
to something so small
but full of love.

our time here is
A THIN, BRITTLE THING.

and i am not willing to spend it
ALREADY HALF-DEAD.

rameses the second

in the dust of a fallen empire,
a shattered statue sun-fades in silence.

he was said to be a pharaoh. his name
meant to reverberate endlessly through time.
an everlasting echo to outlive us all.

but his cities sank into the sand.
his temples crumbled.
the desert reclaimed it.

all that remains is ruins now
and a fragmented face.

a hollow boast.

milk of the tide

and, somehow, i take great comfort in this:
nothing lasts forever. it used to scare me.
but if nothing lasts,
then neither will fear and failure.
regret or shame.
it has a time that will end.

i won't be etched in stone.
and that means i am free to be soft and silly.
to live with mistakes and know that now is all
we really ever have.

ephemeral

the candle will still gutter and drip
whether or not i watch over it.

its wick will still burn
whether or not i fear the flame.

the smoke will still pirouette into nothing
whether or not i try to seize it.

and i will still die one day
whether or not i shrink from living.

what my father taught me

one year, just before christmas,
someone broke into my dad's home
and took everything he owned.

they stole his beloved collector hardbacks,
his father's aged whiskey,
even the box of my baby teeth
from back when fairies were real.

he had every right to be miserable,
but when i wept for him
he only reached for me,
pressed my forehead to his chest.

he had nothing that christmas.
no wrapped presents to give,
or food for guests in his cupboards.
no radio to play the festive jingles.
but he could gift me love and strength.

that was more than enough.

firework or a flood

my first kiss was underneath a willow tree.
his mouth was chocolate mint sweet
with summer ice cream.

i don't remember
the colour of his eyes now.
moments once so sharp and crisp
have clouded over time.

not everything that feels
like a firework or a flood
will always feel so loud.

if i am fortunate enough
to wrinkle and grey,
i think there will be a lot that hurts now
that will mean very little to me later.

where i go to smile

i have this box i keep under my bed.
sometimes, when i need to, i slide it out
from underneath my mattress, slip the lid off.
letters. cards. photographs. dried shoots of lavender
and pressed petals people gifted me over time.
i kept them all.

a time capsule of moments
when others thought of me and poured love
into something and put it in my grasp.
said *yes, you matter.*
keep this—and remember when you forget.

sometimes, when i'm sinking in the high tide,
i visit other peoples' words
when i have no kind ones for myself
and just sit with them a while.

milk of the tide

nanna

on her own birthdays, she'd usher me close
and slip a ribboned gift into my grasp,
something she bought or made herself,
cocooned in cellophane paper and kindness.

she roasted dinners and sent them down,
warm foil parcels of love
when we didn't have much.

she cheers over every achievement.
to her, i am worthy of a parade
for any reason at all.

and the hand-made cards, laced with trimmings,
constellated with glitter and dotted in gems.
even when her fingers stiffen and pain
locks her fingers, she works tirelessly to craft them,
just to give them away.

her love hums beneath my skin.
i hope i can carry even half of it
out into the world.

leeza jayde

today, i met someone new

i pinch this piece of paper that you wrote
your number on between my thumb
and forefinger. paper has never felt so heavy.

but i am comfortable hiding in this crawl space
between hurt and hope.

it's safer here.
safer to wonder
instead of waiting
for you to wander.

but if i'm being honest,
the way you look at me is my achilles' heel.

the thing is, i don't take risks.

i don't wiggle teeth when they're loose.
i slow down at amber lights.

but if i'm still being honest,
you make me want to try.

clearing space

love finds you unexpectant,
wakes something inside.
the spark of embers,
and you wonder if it's too soon,
too much, too dangerous,
because you've been burned before.

since we met, i've been hungry
to know where you grew up,
what your favourite colour is,
your fears. how you got that scar.

without meaning to,
i'm clearing space for you
in all of the corners of my life.

maybe you'll stay,
and maybe you won't,
but i think
i would like to see this through.

i think i'd like to be brave.

leeza jayde

i do not run

it's raining cherry petals
in kyoto again today.
soft, flushed confetti drifting down,
catching in my hair.

i turn left into a bamboo grove
where the air is damp with dew,
and the birds call to each other
between the hush.

you slip your hand in mind,
press your lips to the slope of my neck,
and i remember the days when love
felt like the pulled pin of a grenade.
how i had learned to recoil at tenderness,
mistaking it for a snare.

but here, amongst the green cathedrals of bamboo,
under a heaven raining pink petals around us,
i do not run.

the ache is not a fear,
but something almost
like forgiveness.

milk of the tide

fragmented pieces of who i was—
different hands that held me,
loved me, changed me,
and let go.

seashells swelling with the sound of good times.
shipwrecked fragments of old regrets.
messages in bottles that my childhood self
hoped that i would read and remember
that have finally found me again.

these are the things
that come in with the milk of the tide
lapping at my feet.

i do not have to be a wound
if i choose not to be.

i get to decide
who i will be from here.

leeza jayde

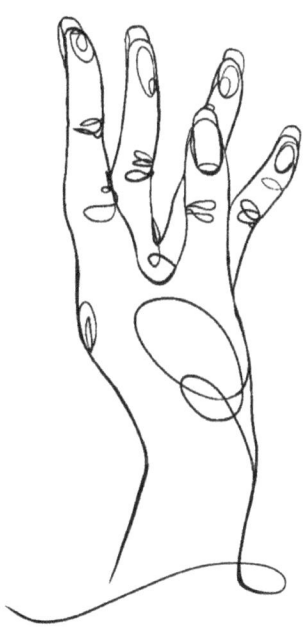

AUTHOR'S NOTE

The relationship-related poems in this collection are inspired by a handful of different loves I have had the privilege, and often the pain, of learning from. Each person—whether brief or lasting in my life—was a pocket of time that left its mark, shaping who I am and how I perceive and navigate the world around me.

This book also grapples with my experience of navigating poor mental and physical health, as well as the profound loss of a friend who took their life. The poems within these pages reflect both the hardship and the healing that have come from these experiences. I hope to remind anyone who might be reading this that you are not alone if you, or someone you know, has felt or feels this way.

If you ever find yourself struggling, please reach out to someone. There are people who care, and there is help available. You are not a burden. You are not asking for too much. Please remember that your story matters. You are enough as you are and you deserve love and support, no matter where you are in your journey. You are worthy.

ACKNOWLEDGEMENTS

Milk of the Tide serves as the prequel to my debut poetry collection, *While We're Here*. By comparison, it's a grittier excavation of some of my most painful experiences and I think it's powerful and cathartic to normalise discussions around poor mental health. Writing the pieces in this project was a moving and vulnerable experience, and I did not undertake this journey alone. I am deeply grateful for the supportive community around me.

Thank you to my readership. There is no greater gift than knowing my poetry has been read and supported by you.

To my mother, father and nanna: I am privileged to be yours. You make me feel loved beyond measure. If I had nothing else, I'd still be rich in that. For Thomas—you will always be my childhood best friend, here or not. For Shirley, Hugh and Pauline; you were always so kind to me. To Paula—my beautiful bonus mother. And for Ashley, my lantern in a dark room. My reason why.

For God and all He has done for me. Thanks will never be enough. It will never even come close.

To Shayla, Kevin and Belle, for not only the valuable,

thorough feedback provided in the early drafting stages of this poetry collection, but for being such dear friends to me over the years.

Courtney, whose hands gave these pages their layered beauty from drawing long into the quiet hours of the night, and whose friendship continues to be a soft presence beside me.

Euan, for his meticulous typesetting and skill, and Rachel for her carefully curated, gorgeous cover design. Thank you both.

My dear Dale, Jess, Cara, Telle, Sara, T., Katie, Simone, Holly, Ty, Emily, Susie, Gene, Shylee, Cass, Harry, Jacob, Tabitha, Kai and Paige, you are all ceaselessly supportive. I'm blessed to know each of you.

And for C.W. You are not gone, my friend.
You are with us still.

ABOUT THE AUTHOR

LEEZA JAYDE is an Australian poet, teacher and mental health awareness advocate whose work is inspired by the quiet magic of everyday life and the depth of the human experience. With honesty, vulnerability and compassion, her poetry explores healing, love's many forms, loss, grief and existentialism. She writes with the hope that her words might help others feel understood, seen and comforted.

When she isn't lost between the pages of a paperback, Leeza shares her words with her growing community on Instagram at @leezajaydepoetry.

WITH SPECIAL THANKS
TO THE ILLUSTRATOR

Courtney Errey is an Australian artist and teacher. She has been drawing since she was old enough to grip a pencil, and specialises in realism, particularly with animals and flora, but enjoys experimenting in various art forms.

You can find her on Instagram under @courtney_errey_art, or at home, cocooned in blankets with hot cup of French Earl Grey, surrounded by her affectionate dog, cat and two birds.

www.ingramcontent.com/pod-product-compliance
Lightning Source LLC
Chambersburg PA
CBHW031444040426
42444CB00007B/964